HOW TO MAKE PEOPLE LAUGH

Learn the Science of Laughter to Make a Powerful Impression, Win Friends and Improve Your Sense of Humour Even If You Don't Think You're Funny

CHRISTOPHER KINGLER

TABLE OF CONTENTS

INTRODUCTION

Many people say, "keep them laughing" and you might think this is as easy as telling a joke. Well, not really. It turns out that there are some secrets to telling jokes. There are certain things you need to do for your joke to get a laugh.

First, be confident with yourself and the joke you're telling. If you seem insecure, nervous, or reluctant to tell it, then they probably won't find it funny at all.

Next, get the timing right. You need to practice with this one so you can get a sense of how long you have from the point you say the punch line to when people laugh, and then you can get your timing down. In telling a joke, timing is everything. The perfect moment for a joke is when everyone is already laughing or they've just finished laughing.

You must be in the right environment to tell a joke.. For example, if you're in a crowded room with strangers, then no one is going to appreciate your jokes. You need the appropriate environment in which to tell people your jokes. The problem with telling jokes in public is that you might make serious mistakes.

If you don't know what to say next after you tell your joke, remember that building up the level of tension while they wait for something funny to happen again will heighten their excitement when it finally does.

This doesn't mean that every time you tell a joke you have to repeat it. Sometimes you can tell a joke once, and it works well. For example, if you have just told a joke about a food item and people ask you what that is, then the best thing to do is just say "Lemons." This hands down will make everyone laugh because the next time they ask, just say "lemons" again.

It is good to know how to tell jokes, and to talk about yourself. It is important to be able to tell a joke and be yourself when you do it.

There may be times in your life when you need to tell a joke, especially if you are among people you know. If the people around you are laughing, then what you're saying is funny. Even if they laugh at something stupid, it's still good because it lets them know you can joke around and be yourself.

This is one of those things that sounds smart, but you don't have to do it. It is recommended, but that's it. You can be funny without telling a joke if you are in the mood to laugh about something that is happening in real life. People around you see that you can tell a joke when they see how funny and genuine you are.

Some people think they know how to tell a joke. They might tell you one that goes on forever, or it is a repeat of a joke that they have heard somewhere else. These are the people you should not listen to. People need to learn the difference between funny and unfunny.

In laughing at a joke that someone else tells, there is much more involved than one would think. The reason people laugh in most situations is that this person has said something that other people agree with or find relevant and they want that person to be rewarded for it.

The reason people laugh is to make other people see it's funny. They view this as a reward.

Some people may not laugh at everything. They might not be in the mood to laugh or they don't agree with the joke. They may have a poor attitude and not want to reward the person for telling the joke or for making fun of another person. Some people might laugh because they are nervous, or are themselves afraid of being laughed at.

One thing to remember when you tell someone a joke, is that no matter how confident you are, never tell your joke until everyone has finished laughing. This is important, because it will prevent you from telling a bad joke that no one laughs at, and never and tell a joke that you think everyone will like. Stick to jokes that are funny to you.

There is nothing wrong with laughing at someone's jokes, but if you do this too much, then they might think that there is something wrong with you.

Even if you get a joke, there are still times when you shouldn't laugh at it. It is important to know which jokes to laugh at and which ones to avoid laughing at because sometimes a person will say something stupid that they think is funny. Don't laugh at such jokes. This will be embarrassing for them.

It's always important to understand when to laugh at a joke and when not to, but there is more to it than that. The way a person laughs reveals if they are laughing for the right reasons or not. Some people will try to laugh at a joke even though they don't get it. This makes them appear to be trying to gain attention.

CHAPTER 1: THE SCIENCE OF LAUGHTER

The science of laughter is as intriguing as it is complex. How laughter impacts our mental and physical health can affect small things, like how much you sleep at night. Innovative studies have shown that humor can provide several positive benefits. So don't be afraid to laugh!

We're going to explain what happens when you laugh, what tickles you, and why not laughing for 10 minutes equals a missed meal break.

Essentially, laughter is an emotional response to something funny, but that's not all. It's more than that, which is why understanding exactly what it can do for you is so important.

Laughter as Medicine

Well-known research on the health benefits of laughter focuses mostly on the physical aspects. The Centers for Disease Control and Prevention (CDC) recognizes laughter as part of a healthy lifestyle. A 2004 report showed that laughter can be beneficial to both your heart and respiratory system.

The way this works is through stress reduction. Laughter is a natural response that releases endorphins. These can help ease stress and promote relaxation. Laughing out loud for no reason or laughing in response to a humorous situation results in endorphin release.

The physical benefits of laughter are as crucial as the mental benefits. A good night's sleep is easier to achieve when you're in a good mood. Stress leads to physical ailments such as muscle breakdown and high blood pressure.

Laughing reduces your body's physiological reactions to stressful situations, and fights symptoms that arise from stress.

The Endorphins

Endorphins are the body's natural opiates and are responsible for feelings of euphoria and general well-being. In short, they elevate mood and block pain. Laughing also releases dopamine. Dopamine is a "feel good" endorphin whose production is triggered when you see or hear something funny.

Endorphins are released even when you laugh for no reason. So the next time you're in a bad mood or in an uncomfortable situation, try to force yourself to laugh about it. You never know what it could do for your emotional state or your health.

Getting Started

If you're just learning about the benefits of laughter, we can relate to you feeling a little confused on where to start. There's a lot of information out there that may seem hard to filter through.

To help you understand how laughter works, we've created some helpful infographics for you. This should help clear up any confusion and give you the basics of what happens when you laugh, why it's important, and what to do about it.

How does laughter work?

- Laughter reduces tension.
- Positive emotions like joy, contentment, or a sense of well-being follow instances of laughter.
- It's the sense of humor that causes the release of endorphins in the body.
- They give you a boost of energy, help you maintain a healthy weight, and help you sleep better at night.
- Laughter is contagious!

CHAPTER 2: WHAT HAPPENS IN YOUR BRAIN?

When you experience humor, your brain releases a chemical called dopamine. Dopamine is the same chemical released during orgasm. In combination with the mental stimulation of a joke, it's possible to experience extreme euphoria.

What Are the Different Types of Humor?

There are many types of humor, however, we will focus on the principal three. Slapstick, sarcasm, and puns. A hearty laugh can come from any or all three types in various combinations.

Sarcasm

"That was hilarious. I almost died laughing. The timing was perfect!"

Sarcasm, through the use of insults, aggression, exaggeration, and contradictions, makes a person (or group of people) look like fools or be seen in a negative light. Sarcasm is very useful if you need to put someone in their place.

Slapstick

"That's not funny."

Slapstick employs the physical to create humor, usually expressed clumsiness, or other physical failures. It requires great timing and concentration. In the middle of the night, a man walks into a bar. The man goes up to the bartender, slurs "Gimme whiskey." The bartender, annoyed by this drunkard, gives him water instead. The drunk looks at his glass of water and says, "This is water. I wanted whiskey." The bartender then throws a glass of whiskey at him, splashing it in the man's face.

Puns

"I'm sure every joke you tell is a real knee-slapper!"

Puns are when you say one word with two meanings, creating an ambiguity. Puns can be difficult to construct, as they require a deep knowledge of the language. For example, "A horse walks into a bar and the bartender says 'Why the long face?'" Everyone knows a horse has an elongated face and this makes this joke funny.

How to Become a Better Joke Writer

Becoming a great joke writer involves lots of trial and error.. Write down your ideas and see if they work. If they don't, try again! Also, you can get ideas from watching television, reading the newspaper, or paying attention to the people around you. The key is paying attention and being willing to listen so that when someone says something funny, you can put it in your back pocket for later use.

How Jokes Work

Jokes have four components–sets-ups, punch lines, responses, and tags. These are vital for a successful joke. The entire joke needs to make sense, but you have more than one chance to make it funny. Try not to get frustrated, and remember, the best jokes are ones that people can't predict!

CHAPTER 3: WORK ON YOUR IMAGE AND DEVELOP INCREDIBLE CHARISMA

Working on your image and developing your charisma puts you on track to being a natural comedian. Practice talking with someone, and as soon as they laugh, make a joke about it. (Remember, if you can't come up with anything right away, just wait for their next line before responding). Try to do it when they're not expecting it—like every three minutes instead of every fifteen seconds! Remember that timing is everything in comedy—timing combined with a sense of humor will get you very far in life.

One of the great things about humor is that the stakes are low. If you can make people laugh at your expense, you'll seem humble and people will appreciate that. Work on your delivery, and have a few different jokes that you can use in social situations.

Sometimes there's nothing funnier than a good prank... and there's no finer art than the practical joke. Keep in mind that practical jokes rarely work unless they're subtle. Practical jokes are often more satisfying than cracking a good joke.

Making someone laugh is a great feeling! Laughter is infectious! It's an incredible thing to get someone to laugh at something and great fun to see people laughing together—even better when they are unaware that you're behind the laughter.

Be careful, know when to draw the line. You need to know that your audience welcomes your humor before pushing it too far.

If you can make people laugh, you're all but guaranteed to garner everyone's affection. Be careful though, you don't want people to think that you're arrogant.

The ability to make someone laugh is a gift! If you have this gift, use it wisely. Think about the type of humor that will work best in your particular situation and be careful not to offend anyone. Make every joke count!

When all else fails...

If all else fails and you can't think of anything funny to say, turn to the best joke book I've ever found: "Chicken Soup for the Teenage Soul: The Real Deal."

Now that you know how to make people laugh, the next step is learning some jokes. There are millions and millions of jokes out there (not all are funny). You'll have to try out a few and see what you think of them. Start with your favorites, it's a learning process.

Now you're on your way to being a natural comedian! It takes years to learn how to be funny, so if you're thinking of getting into comedy, give up now. You'll only embarrass yourself... that is, unless you're really good.

Remember that timing is everything in comedy—timing combined with a sense of humor will get you very far in life.

CHAPTER 4: IMPROVE YOUR HUMOR AND PERSONALITY

Improve your humor and personality with these five easy tips!

The number one way to spice up your sense of humor is to paying attention to what makes you chuckle, while reading an article or looking at a meme. What made you laugh the most? What made you laugh the least? Asking yourself those questions may help pinpoint what kind of humor works best for you.

Many people like puns, but not everyone. Jokes and puns can be too cheesy or clever. If that's what floats your boat, it's probably best to stick with that, but if not, try translating the sentiment into another form to see if it works better for you.

When you create a new joke, examine it. Was it corny? If so, why did that make you laugh? This may be a form of humor that works well for you. If it was too dry, too intellectual, then maybe you could build it a differently by adding emotion or action.

Improve your personality by trying to use different voices and personas. It takes practice, but once you get into it, you might find yourself doing more than just talking back to the characters on TV! Record yourself doing different impressions, such as movie villains, cartoon characters, or famous people.

CHAPTER 5: THE ART OF SELF-DEPRECATING

Self-deprecating humor is an art. It is about not taking one's self too seriously, and even making fun of one's self. There are three steps to becoming a great self-deprecator.

1. Pick a personal trait that you're insecure or embarrassed by, such as being bald, being short, having acne scars, or being poor.
2. Introduce yourself as though you were talking to someone meeting you for the first time and is unaware of your insecurity or embarrassment (imagine speaking to your date for the first time). Is your insecurity or embarrassment at all evident to your date? Does your date notice anything that makes you feel awkward or uncomfortable? If so, you're on the right track. If not, talk to someone who knows you and can make suggestions.
3. With each joke or other self-deprecating remark, use the phrase "You know me." Be sure to echo it in a mocking tone of voice. For example: "You know me! I'm short, bald, and overweight"

Step 1 should be taken up when preparing your material for delivery. Step 2 is a practice step. Step 3 is the delivery step.

Some people find it easier to make fun of themselves than others. Comedians often rely on self-deprecating humor because it's much easier (and safer) to make fun of yourself rather than someone else. The 3 steps above are a formulaic way of doing it, but can't be applied universally. One must be creative and let one's personality come through in the material. A good way to get started is to write ten ways in which you are awkward or embarrassing, then come up with ten "You know me!" jokes or remarks to match each trait.

The important thing to remember while practicing this art is to not take yourself too seriously. If you do, you risk pricking your bubble of self-esteem. You enjoy greater success in dealing with your feelings of insecurity if you can make fun of them. Making jokes related to your insecurities should make it easier for the people around you to see how foolish they are and not take themselves so seriously.

A person who has learned how to make self-deprecating humor can use his or her skills in everyday life and in social situations. They can use these skills to diffuse tense situations, and to show people they are not overly serious about certain things.

For example, let's say you just been dumped. You are now paying all the bills. You are now speaking to someone you're attracted to. Using self-deprecating humor will diffuse tension and act as a confidence booster for your date. You can end up with your date thinking, "This guy has no ego!"

Self-deprecation can be in business dealings. When meeting people for the first time, a self-deprecating comedian can never be too sure about how people will react to self-deprecation. They must be prepared to "go with the flow" and not take things too seriously. For instance, you are meeting someone for the first time, introduce yourself and find out that they like your sense of humor. They tell you they know someone who is like you. You ask “Who?” and they say, “A guy I know.” You reply as if you’re self-deprecating: “You KNOW me!” Everyone likes to feel good about what they say. The comedian who admits he or she is a little insecure while making other people feel good makes the interaction more positive for all parties involved, not just for themselves.

Self-deprecating humor shows you are not too serious about things, and that you can laugh at yourself. It shows you are not egotistical or stuck up. Self-deprecating humor is one of the most important tools in the toolbox of successful comedians.

CHAPTER 6: TURN YOUR BIO INTO A FUNNY STORY

Turn your bio into a funny story with these thirty ideas.

1. I'm a high-functioning alcoholic.
2. I passed out in the bathtub and drowned.
3. The other day, I accidentally ate a ham sandwich that had mayonnaise on it.
4. My favorite song is "Crazy Frog Goes Pop" by Crazy Frog (featuring samples of JT).
5. These days, the only time people want to hear my opinions is when they ask what time it is or where the toilet paper is kept.
6. My favorite color is.
7. Every Valentine's Day, I send my wife a card saying, "Love, Your Husband."
8. I was robbed the other day.
9. When I was born, the doctors couldn't wait to unwrap me from my mummy.
10. Recently, my dog started barking uncontrollably at a taxidermy horse in our living room.
11. My neighbor told me that for a man of his age, he sure has some magnificent hair.

12. My wife is such a bitch that she won't let me smoke in the house–if I wanted to smoke out of doors I'd have married something with gills.
13. Seasonal allergies have me sneezing like a choo-choo train.
14. I have an aquarium at home with only two fish how the third fish got in there, I don't know.
15. My mother encouraged me to get into show business, so I became a ventriloquist.
16. I'm not very photogenic.
17. When I was a kid, my parents told me that if people talked badly about you, it meant that they were jealous of you. It didn't really work, though–I went to middle school and was the most hated kid there.
18. I was recently voted "least likely to succeed."
19. When I was a child, people told me that the stars were the same stars as we had here on earth. I believed them–until I got older and realized that they were all different.
20. There is an "I love you" for everybody–some people just don't know where to look for it, or when to listen for it.
21. The first time I shaved, it felt like someone else's face.
22. My wife thought it would be nice if we could have a kid together, so she bought some baby bottles and left them out on the counter.
23. I took a shower in the gym yesterday, so I'm all sweaty.
24. My wife has me on my back 24 hours a day.
25. The other day, I was driving my car along the highway with the windows rolled up when a group of squirrels jumped out in front of me and startled me half to death.

26. Even my family members don't respect me—so what do they talk about when they're together?
27. No one has ever heard me give the "thumbs up" sign.
28. My son's first word was "asshole."
29. My wife wants me to get a job, but I don't want to get a job.
30. I'm going to make sure that my eyes are open when they ship me off to Iraq.

CHAPTER 7: EXERCISES

Exercises to make your face look funny:

1. Put on your tightest fitting rubber bands, then stretch your mouth over a tennis ball and hold it there for the next 5 minutes.
2. Place the tennis ball inside an empty plastic container, then wet it with water to activate its stickiness. Now you can put a small grape on top of the rubber band and let it slowly slide down as you go about your day!
3. Apply spicy sauce to either side of your lip, gradually making them spicier and spicier until you reach whatever level is tolerable for you (I recommend starting with 4 drops).
4. Place a weak smile on your face with a small piece of tape and have a friend take a picture of you. You'll end up with one wide-open eye and one half closed.
5. Spitting into the middle of the street will make everyone on the sidewalk laugh at you because it's hilarious!
6. Spend ten minutes in front of a mirror, pulling on your face until it looks like you've been crying for one hour, then cry and wipe your tears on your sleeve for another 5 minutes. Then cry some more.
7. I don't know how to explain this one, just rub your tongue along the roof of your mouth until it bleeds a bit.

8. Drink a can of soda with no ice in it, then go for a 30-minute run, finally finishing with a bout of violent coughing and vomiting. You'll look like you've been laughing for hours.
9. Spend one hour covering yourself in baby powder with your hands or a towel, then drive down to the lake and wade in as far as you can before you completely sink beneath the surface.
10. Remove a very strong toothpick from the back of your mouth, tie it to a piece of string, and hang it outside in the wind.
11. Put 3 rubber bands around your face and pull them apart slowly until an expression of rage appears.
12. Put all the spaces in between every word on this page into this sentence and make it rhyme: "I am so funny."
13. In public, while performing with your improved troupe, take out a pen, start furiously scribbling on notebook paper for a few minutes. Immediately afterward, erase everything you wrote, then scribble again. Continue this until you're off-script and the audience gives you a startled gasp. Giggle to yourself as if it's the best joke ever told.
14. When going through security at the airport (with a completely clean body), ask an agent if he knows what you look like under your uniform before proceeding to unbutton the top two buttons of your shirt and scrunch up your face in anticipation of his reply regarding the security pat down.
15. During a stand-up comedy act, put one leg up on a chair and slowly rock from side to side while laughing hysterically until the audience is completely baffled by your performance.
16. After drinking a cup of water, slurp it up one nostril at a time and let it dribble out the other before continuing with your day.

17. When you have to sneeze, make sure that you do so without covering your mouth or nose and when the moment comes to sneeze out those initial contractions, make sure you hold perfectly still with your chin tilted upwards and keep your eyes closed until the sneeze happens in its entirety.
18. Listen to a recording of yourself laughing on tape for ten minutes (or until the tape runs out). Scream into a mirror in front of you while watching yourself laugh through that reflection.
19. Walk up to a group of people and say "Hi, my name is Andrew," laugh inappropriately loud, then blink your eyes twice slowly without speaking another word.
20. Wear loose pants, then hitch them up as far as you can while making sure the entire world can see your underwear.
21. As you're typing an email on your computer, loudly and obnoxiously fart several times fixing no errors and let out a hearty chuckle.
22. Once you have the attention of a friend or coworker, lean your chin in towards your chest and make eye contact with them while keeping that awkward expression.
23. Lick your hand, then throw it up and wave it around until somebody grabs onto it.
24. Grab a tree branch, hang upside down from it for five minutes (making sure nobody sees), then crawl to the ground and walk away saying nothing to anyone.
25. Ask someone for one hundred pennies, then offer to give them one penny back if they can guess which hand they're in before the penny is removed from their grasp.

26. See how many different laughs you can produce in a row without taking a breath.
27. When you're eating alone, put your hands over your face and pretend that you're talking to someone who isn't there.
28. Take off all of your clothes and ask if anyone wants to play naked volleyball with you at the beach!
29. Go to a fast-food restaurant and order $15 worth of food at a drive-thru window, then hand them one penny and walk away while laughing loudly one foot from their car window.
30. Write yourself a note saying "DO NOTHING. FOR THE REST OF YOUR LIFE." Sign the note with your name, then put it in a frame on your mantel. Every morning when you wake up, read the note aloud to yourself and pretend that you're taking it seriously.
31. Pull out a pair of swim goggles and put them on while at a public pool. Jump off the diving board wiping out ridiculously hard, and hitting your head on the bottom causing some dizziness to occur.
32. Fill an empty spray bottle with water then use it to douse yourself with some water before doing so.
33. Write a note to yourself and have it on your person. As you're getting ready to leave the house for the day, ask yourself why you wrote that note. Then, start laughing uncontrollably before saying aloud "Oh snap."
34. When walking through any area with lots of people, every so often make random noises while talking out loud in an obnoxious manner.

35. Whenever you're out in public and notice that there are very few people around, point at yourself and say "I'm invisible!" slowly, then run away from somebody holding a camera phone or pointing their phone at you without looking back.
36. Do the "umbrella dance" at a party.
37. Next time you're walking down the street, throw your arms out and start making a funny face as though you're possessed.
38. Walk up to someone and ask if they know how to get to Wonderland, then walk away laughing hysterically while saying "Gotcha!" repeatedly until you get into your car or home.
39. Make your phone ring in public by pulling out the battery.
40. Whenever someone is walking at a normal pace, start running towards them full speed and yell "Oooohhh... Ka-BOOM!" before they see you coming up behind them.
41. Walk around for a few minutes in front of your local Walmart store, then jump up and down on one leg while repeatedly saying "Dollar?" while holding up a single dollar bill as if it's a prize to win every time you say it.
42. Whenever you see someone on a plane, bus, or in the airport acting like they don't have enough legroom, walk over and say "I've got plenty of room!" while spreading your legs as wide open as possible.
43. Whenever you're walking down the street and hear someone ask for directions to somewhere you don't know how to get to, give them incorrect directions or pretend to not know where they want to go.

44. Start walking around in public with a carrot hanging from your nose or a cucumber sticking out of your pants pocket and act like it's normal.
45. Start humping random objects in public, and when someone asks you why you're acting weird, say "I'm just playing with my food."
46. Walk your pet on a leash in public and then carry the leash over your shoulder like it's a gun.
47. Start carrying around a sign that reads "Free food" or "Free money" whenever you see a homeless person.
48. Whenever walking down the street with someone else, hold up one finger and cross the other foot over it while saying "Did I pass gas?"
49. Whenever walking down the street with someone else, either whisper to them or giggle when they talk to you.
50. Deep sigh loudly when you are alone.
51. Tell dirty jokes frequently and tell them as if they were profound observations about the human condition.
52. Call people smart, sexy, cool, stupid, ugly, and fat.
53. Borrow money from a friend then never pay it back or pay it back five years later and act like you don't know what they are talking about when they bring it up.
54. Pick your nose in public over three times per day for no reason other than to gross people out.
55. When someone goes to shake your hand, pull a gun out of your waistband and point it at their head and say, "Whoops!"
56. Wear Crocs® in public.

57. When you're at the table with your family, say "What? WHY ARE YOU ALL STARING AT ME?!"
58. Stand up in the middle of a conversation with someone and shout, "WHY DO WE LIVE ON THIS PLANET ANYWAY?! TAKE ME TO OUTER SPACE!"
59. Get yourself extra tickets to sporting events from work or classmates by pretending they were meant for another purpose all along.
60. When the movie ends, ask if anyone else wants to stay and watch the credits.
61. Tell people that if they don't laugh at your new jokes, you're going to kill them.
62. Own a white belt with a big red buckle and wear it constantly for no reason other than to annoy people who try to ask you what you're doing with it on your waist.
63. Be rude to everybody in public by acting as though they have offended you.
64. When you find a sweet potato while on a hike, throw it at random people and act like you didn't do it.
65. When asked for your name, say "The name is whatever gives the person the most pleasure."
66. Tell people that your life was going to be better than theirs unless they laugh very hard at everything you say.
67. Ask people if they know who Bruce Lee is, even if you know perfectly well that they do.

68. Whenever you're done with something, start re-doing it again until it's perfect or until someone tells you to stop doing it and leave them alone.
69. Ask random people if they can speak a certain language even though you know they can't.
70. Tell everyone within earshot of you that the object you are holding is a rare, precious artifact from outer space and that it is worth thousands of dollars.
71. Walk up to people and ask them if they are "the one."
72. Walk around with an old Walkman on your head and pretend like it's giving you advice about your life choices or what to say next after every single thing you say out loud.
73. Walk around with an old pocket watch in public and pretend that it's a cell phone.
74. In the middle of a meeting or conversation, abruptly ask someone if they remember "that one guy who said that thing."
75. Laugh uncontrollably at someone when they are talking to you and give no rational reason.
76. Walk up to somebody at random and ask them if their whole family has been killed yet because you have some information to share with them relevant to whatever it is they're doing while acting as though it's the most important information anyone has ever shared with you before.
77. Go to a stranger's house and start talking about the weather and how nice it looks outside.
78. Every time you answer the phone, ask, "Who is this?"

79. Eat an entire bag of Sour Patch Kids and then constantly ask people if they are enjoying them.
80. Try to be offended whenever someone makes fun of your appearance or something you're wearing, even when you know that they only did it because they thought it was funny at the moment or because they are insecure about their appearance.
81. Say "um" non-stop in a conversation until you run out of things to say and make yourself seem like an idiot in doing so.
82. Whenever you get mad at someone, start telling them they're a dick head and that they deserve to be treated like one.
83. Tell people you've seen their dog on your neighbor's lawn and keep telling them that until they believe you.
84. Go to an abandoned house or some other place where there is no one else around you and practice kung-fu moves or punches right in front of it while saying "I'm so good! I'm the best!" repeatedly in a goofy voice.
85. At Walmart, count every single blue thing in the store.
86. Pick your nose and start talking about how great it tastes and how you wish you could get a whole glass of it.
87. When people say "hey" to you, say "Hey! What's up?" right back at them in an enthusiastic voice, like they were waiting for you to come over to their place all along.
88. Whenever someone asks for your opinion on something, laugh out loud because of how absurd it is that anyone would ever want to hear your opinion on the matter.
89. Start telling people they're being too serious about something and should just get with the program and have some fun.

90. Go up to a police officer while wearing a dark-colored trench coat and ask them if you look like a criminal before trying to buy drugs from them.
91. Tell everyone at work that you were jealous of how well-dressed they were for work today so you went out and bought new clothes just for the occasion even though it is unrealistic for someone to spend that much money on new clothes for one day when money is tight.
92. Start talking with yourself as if you were a movie character full of wise and humorous observations.
93. Go to a gas station and start screaming "Come on down! Make my day, come on down!" repeatedly while holding out your arms like you're expecting someone to jump into them from across the street.
94. Go up to random people in public and ask them "Do you believe in vampires?" when they look as though they're asking you that same question.
95. Tell people you can't wait to get old because you'll be able to do whatever you want without worrying about what any of your friends or family members think and act like it's the most liberating feeling in the world.
96. Whenever someone asks you what day it is, ask them if they're sure that they need to know that right this second.
97. Tell people to stop staring at you and that it's rude for them to keep looking at your face when there are other things around them at all times.
98. Whenever you see someone walking around with a cute animal, ask them if they found it on the street.

99. Tell people you are in alliances with everyone in the world as long as they're not trying to kill you at that very minute.
100. Start telling people everything you do is a conspiracy for your enjoyment that benefits no one else but yourself and your family, even though it hurts most of the people around you who care about you.

CHAPTER 8:
KNOW YOUR AUDIENCE

Know your audience. Have a sense of what the people you are trying to make laugh are interested in. Find out what they find funny by asking them questions and listening to their answers.

For example, if you have a friend who loves dogs, try telling jokes about dogs or telling stories about funny things that happen with your dog.

Keep a sense of humor in mind when it comes to making people laugh. You should take into consideration that people often laugh for different reasons than you might think.

For example, if you are telling a joke to your friend about how dumb college students are, this might be funny to you because you find college students annoying. However, this joke may not be funny to your friend who is going to college!

Avoid telling jokes that can make people uncomfortable or offended. People dislike being around others who make them feel uneasy.

Don't force yourself on other people. Don't try too hard to make them laugh. It isn't worth it and it will most likely backfire on you.

Think of what makes other people laugh and use it in the situations in which you need to make them laugh. Write down your observations and try to use them the next time you are trying to make people laugh.

Try to connect with others. People are most likely to laugh when they feel like they have a connection or bond with the person who is making them laugh. You can create this bond by jokes that relate closely to things shared between you and your audience (e.g., school, childhood, dating).

You can also build a relationship by sharing things about yourself that others don't know and then proceed with funny jokes that relate to the information you have just given away, thus creating a sense of closeness between you and the audience.

Don't just use joke routines to get laughs and then move on. Try to incorporate your jokes into the conversation. This will give the audience a sense of being part of the experience by sharing in your humor and laughing along with you.

Try "cold reading" for jokes. Cold reading is a method in which comedians use their natural intuition to convince people into believing them, often leading them to reveal personal information about themselves that they might not otherwise choose to reveal, such as their weight, marital status, or political views.

Cold reads can help you get people laughing because it is at least partly based on personalities, which makes it easier for people to laugh at your jokes. Consider asking your audience if they have a couple of friends who are about the same age. Your average listener will probably share a few stories with their friends about their lives and experiences with other people in their lives. This will make it much easier for you to start cold reads on people in your audience.

Here are some actual cold reads:

- “How many feckless teenagers docs it take to conduct an orchestra? None, they can’t read!”
- “Everyone looks younger than they really are, but being young is still better than being old.”
- “I predict that by the time you’re my age, you’ll be willing to do anything for sex. If that’s the case, you’ll be sick of it by now. Why would you want to get older if that means giving up sex?”
- “You have an impressive figure for a woman your age. What are you doing to keep it looking good? (giggle)”

The above cold reads are examples of how to insert these jokes into situations in which people need to laugh.

Have confidence in what you do. When making people laugh, they will need to believe that the jokes are coming from a genuinely funny source for them to be funny. Improve your performance by standing up straight and presenting yourself confidently. Practice your delivery–become a wonderful storyteller.

Ask for feedback if you think your jokes aren’t funny. If you have friends who will give constructive input, ask them for advice. Most people who want to laugh will be open to hearing what friends have to say about what’s funny or not funny. Ask them what they like and don’t like about your jokes so that you can improve and get more laughs!

Practice jokes in different situations. Even if a joke may not be appropriate for every occasion, practicing it regularly will make it natural for when you need it. If you are in a situation where you need to make someone laugh, you will have a joke ready you know will work!

Don't obsess about making people laugh. Don't put so much stress on yourself that you fail. If your primary objective aim is fun and laughter, then relax and enjoy the moment.

Be willing to use humor in moments where it might be inappropriate. It might be awkward, but in serious situations lightening the mood with a funny comment or joke may give others the idea that there is nothing to worry about.

Keep it simple when trying to make people laugh. If you are trying to tease someone, the joke should be as simple as possible, so they can quickly figure out what you are trying to say. If there are too many layers or complexities your joke, it may not be able to stand on its own.

Know the difference between an honest and an unfunny joke. It is much easier to make someone laugh with a joke that is based on something true or real rather than something completely false or imaginary. Try using jokes that involve yourself, so you can relate to them better, and give them more of personal touch (as opposed to making up an entire story about another person).

Poke fun at yourself. People are much more willing to laugh when the joke is about you, as opposed to someone else.

Be ready for jokes that don't go well. If you are trying to make people laugh and they don't give any signs of laughter, don't just stop. Keep telling the joke differently until it gets picked up or understood by someone in your audience.

Make jokes that are short and sweet! Don't try to be too funny or come up with a long story that requires a lot of setups, because it will be harder for people to follow along with you.

Don't rely on props or gimmicks. It is very easy to get too caught up in the props you are using and lose sight of the actual joke, making it boring.

Try to make your humor gender-neutral for maximum appeal. People will appreciate a joke that can be appreciated by both genders.

Don't be afraid of being funny when it comes to the ladies. If you want to make the ladies laugh, try not to rely on gender jokes or gestures that may insult the women in your crowd.

Keep it clean! If people find something offensive in your jokes, they will most likely walk away.

Tell short jokes, not long ones. If you keep telling long jokes, people will lose interest.

Know when to stop telling a joke. If someone has stopped laughing at your joke and it seems like no one else is listening, chances are that your audience has had enough of it and needs to get some fresh air. Try starting over with another one!

Be creative when determining what makes a good joke! Don't rely on the classic punch line. If the audience is already laughing at your story, you will be hard-pressed to make them laugh again with a typical punch line.

Everyone, regardless of age, loves a practical joke. If it can be done in front of friends or family with a little of preparation, people will appreciate the show of creativity. This is something you shouldn't overthink. Just be sure you have enough food for everyone involved in the practical joke!

To achieve this kind of magic with your practical jokes, use these tips:

- Make sure everyone is present before you begin.
- Bring as many props as needed to make it as spectacular as possible.
- Make sure you know what to expect from your audience. If there are children around, make sure adults are involved. Don't scare the children!

We all need of a good laugh. If we take a rest from our everyday troubles and laugh at the fun pranks, we feel better and think more clearly. We may even have an easier time performing the best pranks in the world! Of course, you will not want to cause serious harm or endanger anyone, so be careful! Be certain you know what you're doing if you decide to prank someone. Have fun with your practical jokes!

CHAPTER 9: KNOW THE ANATOMY OF A JOKE

Joke Categories

Jokes can be grouped into categories. The most common categories are:

- Gags, one-line jokes that startle to make the audience laugh. For example, "What do you call a fish with no eyes?" The punchline is usually a pun or play on words.
- Practical jokes are often characterized by tricking someone into doing something embarrassing, yet viewed as funny by their peers. These are often very elaborate and complex plans that will require careful preparation for the prankster to execute them correctly and convincingly. Before a practical joke can be set up, the perpetrator must put the victim at ease and convince them there is no danger in what they are about to do.. A practical joke may involve an element of childish malice in which an innocent act will produce a humiliating experience.
- Costumery (dress up) has its roots in theatrical performances. Costumes are worn to create a hilarious effect.
- A pun is a play on words, relying heavily on word association to make the audience laugh–for example, "Why did the golfer lose his balance?" Answer: "He was clubbed by an irate gopher."

Puns are often used in comedy routines and sitcoms, and are useful in making people laugh when used effectively. The pun may have been invented in the fourth century BC by the Greek poet Cratinus (ca. 429 BC), who amused audiences by mixing two dissimilar dialects of Greek. Punning is an integral part of the Anglo-Saxon heritage and remains popular today in various guises such as spoonerisms, malapropisms, and homophonic puns.

- A joke about a person's name may be a reference to or denigrating comment about their appearance, intelligence, personality, or some other quality. For example, "I had a teacher once who was named George. She was an English major. She taught literature, and she taught me how to spell words."
- A stereotype joke highly depends on the idea that certain groups of people are associated with particular traits, and are usually used as an insult or put down. This is common in some cultures and unacceptable in others.
- A list joke is a short humorous list of things usually in sequential order. Lists of this nature provide a quick, easy laugh. A common example is the "Top 10 Things..." gag, which always ends with, "You Don't Want to Know About!" Another example, Peter Kay made his list jokes famous when he produced the hit DVD series "Live at the Top of the Tower."
- A punny joke uses wordplay to make an audience laugh, such as "I love long walks, especially when they are taken by people who annoy me."
- A setup line leads into a punchline. For example: "If you're lucky, you'll meet a girl with a sense of humor. But don't be disappointed if it's your brother."

- Sight gags are jokes told simply for the sake of making the audience laugh. Some jokes are necessarily visual but can work on other senses throughout the storyline—for example, a line may start with "What does an elephant dream about?" and then end with "As he trudges along..."
- A play on words is a form of humor that uses multiple meanings of a word, or similar-sounding words with dissimilar meanings, to create a humorous effect.
- A joke that relies on the concept of irony to create humor is called an irony joke. Irony involves stating the opposite of what you mean, usually for humorous purposes. For example: "Dad always likes it when Mum doesn't wear her glasses because he says she looks prettier."
- A practical joke, often abbreviated as 'prank', is a mischievous trick played on someone, usually causing the victim to experience embarrassment, perplexity, confusion, or discomfort. Practical jokes differ from confidence tricks or hoaxes in that the victim finds out, or is let in on the joke. A person who performs a practical joke is called a "practical joker."
- One classic form of humor consisting of multiple associated sketches/stories centered on one simple idea. The stories usually take something familiar and present it in an unfamiliar way, often using surrealism or non-sequiturs to achieve this effect—for example, two men are talking while walking down the street. They pass a small dog, then one of them says, "That's not a dog, that's my wife!"
- A joke where the punchline primarily derives its humor from being disgusting or offensive is called a sick joke (or cringe

comedy). For example: "I've got bad news for you... you've got cancer." A common theme of sick jokes is vomit and vomiting (being sick). As this topic is sensitive to many people, these types of jokes are usually not told at parties or in public.

- A joke that employs self-irony is self-derogatory humor. It's a form of satire used to convey a particular point of view and is often used in comedy as a source of character development and continuity. For example: "I'm not ugly... at least, I think."
- Novelty humor frequently makes use of puns, antonyms, spoonerisms, non-sequiturs, or gibberish. A pun involves using a word in one sense when another word that sounds similar has a different meaning–for example: "You left your alibi at the scene of the crime." Puns are common in comic strips where space is limited.
- A joke that uses exaggeration and parody to create humor is satire. It often pushes the boundaries of decency by criticizing social conventions, institutions, or authority figures. Actual people and misdeeds can be used as material for satire. Often, alternative names are needed to clarify that what is being satirized is not real (for example, when a newspaper satirizes the private lives of celebrities).
- A joke that depends upon local knowledge or cultural identity to be funny is called an "ethnic" joke. It is a type of joke that ethnic minorities use, often without realizing it. It usually refers to shared experiences or knowledge specific to the group. Ethnic jokes are not considered good taste when told outside of their specific group.

Puns are also used in other languages to lighten the language of those that embrace the culture. For example, in ice hockey, a player who scores a goal while passing the puck to another player is called a "hat trick" (where "hat" refers to the hockey uniform), and in Spanish, an individual who scores three goals in one game is considered as having performed a "hat-trick."

In Italy for example, the expression "*cravatta di nonna*" (grandmother's scarf), which means something like "scarf," "necklace," or "charm" is used in a jocular way to refer to something old and unusual but of good quality.

These examples explain how puns are a natural way to associate a sound with something that may not have the same meaning or purpose. Individuals that use puns are called "punsters" and they can be very creative when they use words.

Puns are often used to create comedy through the juxtaposition of different parts of speech. For example, a pun can be created by putting two words together that sound alike, but have completely different meanings. The word "punny" is a play on words of "punny" meaning both funny and pathetic.

Lip reading is also used as part of many jokes. It is known as "charm reading," "personality reading," or facial expression reading. A pun is created when it is assumed that the person talking is telling a joke when in fact the person is telling them something completely unrelated. A joke can be created from a lip reader's misunderstanding by leading them to believe a person is saying one thing and they are talking about something completely different, such as, "I just got my hair cut and I'm all shiny."

How Jokes Work

There are three parts to a joke, a setup, a punchline, and a resolution. The setup prepares the story or action so the punchline will make sense. It provides enough information for you to get what's going on in the joke but nothing too specific. The punchline is what's funny about the joke but it also bears similarity to what was just said for it to be considered a "comic twist" rather than a coincidence. Finally, the ending that ties everything together, makes everything fit into place, and comes to an acceptable conclusion. A great joke has the audience laughing so hard during the setup they don't realize what a good joke it is until the punchline. The resolution, on the other hand, is where the audience sees how crazy you are, causing them to laugh again because they were not expecting what came next.

How to Be Funny

Do you know how funny you are? It doesn't matter. You can never tell, but it does matter that you recognize a truly funny comedian. If you can recognize what makes a comedian funny, then you can use that for yourself.

Some comedians are genuinely funny, and use many of the techniques above. If we know how to be funny like them, we can make our jokes that much better. However, there is one major factor governing how funny we can be as a comedian–the audience's frame of mind.

Imagine telling a joke in front of an audience that wants to laugh. The room is filled with smiling faces and everyone seems like they are ready for some great jokes (maybe it is even a comedy club). Now imagine you're telling the same joke in front of the same crowd, but everyone is tired, hungry, or angry. No one is looking for a good time, and they are no longer interested in listening. It's not that they can't laugh at jokes anymore, it's that they don't feel like laughing.

It may take practice to tell how the audience feels and adjust your material accordingly. You can never tell exactly what your audience wants, but knowing if people are tired or hungry can help you give them what they want.

Some people are just naturally funny. Though this will never change (and it makes them hard to teach), you can believe that if you're already a good comedian, then it will only improve with practice and time.

What is funnier than an average joke? A great joke, of course! The key to a great joke is that the twist sent up by the comedian must be completely unexpected to the audience. If your audience knows what's coming, then they will know how it ends. A great joke teller is being able to say what they want when they want, and get a laugh.

A joke is more than just a foolish play on words or topical reference. A joke is an art form that takes time to master. From physical comedy to observational humor, many different comedy styles can be used to make people laugh.

Good comedians can take any slice of life and put it on stage. They use their experiences in life and translate them into material that will keep a crowd laughing for hours.

Comedy Technique

Comedy technique consists of several elements, such as timing and comedic pauses, for which there is no universal formula. The following are tips that comedians have found helpful.

- Stay consistent with your tone of voice when delivering jokes. Whether you're happy or sad, angry or calm, you want to stay in the same mode throughout your punchlines and setups to establish a connection with your audience.
- Don't overuse one type of joke. Try using multiple types in a variety of styles because it'll be more difficult for audiences to predict what's coming next. If you are known for one type of joke, don't risk being too predictable.
- Use natural pauses, and don't be afraid to look down at your notes. You want to suspend the action as much as possible so that your audience can fully appreciate the joke. While it's fine to break between jokes for a second or two, you should do that sparingly and with purpose.
- A key element is to have an interesting angle, which takes a joke in a direction that is different, and not simply a variation of the same joke.
- Being too original can be a detriment to your act. Being slightly obscure, or offbeat might seem smart at first, but audiences can get turned off if it goes on too long.
- Don't try to get the biggest laugh in a way that doesn't relate to the rest of your act because it is a "kill your darlings moment" if they don't laugh.
- Stay away from using a lot of "negative" humor. These jokes are mean-spirited most of the time.

- Don't go overboard with alcohol or drugs before a show. There's nothing worse than having a great joke and then forgetting an entire section of it. It will cause you to stumble through the rest of your act. Of course, some people won't listen when they're intoxicated, so you're on your own with that one!
- Link your jokes together in a cohesive flow. Jokes that are related feel like they're progressing naturally from one to the other, like a short story rather than just random comedy bits thrown together.
- Don't be lazy with your jokes. Make each one as interesting as possible by describing events in great detail, instead of just rattling off the typical "A, B, C" structure. Give people enough information to visualize what's going on.
- Finally, focus on the relationship between substance and style. Avoid becoming consumed with getting laughs at the expense of the original idea you wanted to convey. Otherwise you'll sound like every other comedian saying whatever you can think of that might get a laugh rather than focusing on making a point and giving the audience something valuable.

What Else Do You Have to Say About Comedy?

It is important to learn from others who have been in the business for a long time. It's important to watch and listen to other comedians because that will help you learn how they present their material and their jokes. The best time to approach them is at open mics or shows, but it should be done with a symbiotic mindset and not a predatory one.

- It's important to listen to them, talk with them about how they are doing their shows, and what has worked for them. You don't need to ask them for advice, but you need to be willing to listen if it is offered.

- Use this spirit of learning and asking questions when you practice your act before shows or open mics. This is the best way to learn and improve yourself.
- Finally, seek a group of people who will help you with your material until you're comfortable with it in front of a crowd. The better your jokes are when you deliver them, the better the performance will be. If you have a friend who is a stand-up comedian, get them to help with practice runs of your act and spend time with you and your friends discussing jokes before you go on stage.

Can You Explain What Differentiates Good Comedy From Bad?

I would say it's as simple as knowing what type of jokes work for the situation and knowing how to deliver them powerfully. The key to comedy writing is being able to tell a story that has dramatic effect or perspective. Keep in mind that a good joke is more about the story you're telling than what you say. If someone asks, "So, what's your story?" then you need to dig down deep on the events in your life before the punch line and explain the situations that shaped who you are.

How Important Is It for a Comedian to Write Their Material?

You must write your own material. Writing your own jokes helps with motivation and allows you to learn style and technique.

What Do You Think Makes a Joke Funny?

Is it timing? Is it delivery? A punchline? A well-timed pause? A double-take? A dick joke? The key to comedy, for me, and probably most of the world is relatability. If I can relate to something you just said or did, then I will find it funny.

I'm from New Jersey and I've always gotten a lot of shit for it. I remember reading a bit from Louis CK in which he made fun of the Pennsyltucky accent and how simple it is. He said something to the effect, "if someone asks for directions, you just say, "Go down a piece and they'll know where they're going." There is no greater example of that than my hometown of Millville, NJ. My friend's grandma is a perfect example. They're simple people, but very aware that the rest of the world can't understand what they're saying. It's like an inside joke that creates a distance between outsiders and natives.

Any Advice for People Just Starting?

Much of the advice that helped me get started is old, but still true. You need to be confident in yourself and not try to be too cool for school. You need to go in with a plan. Try to know the audience, know the venue, and know your material.

Do You Have Any Advice for People Wanting to Become Better Comedians?

Just do it. The best way to get good at anything is by doing it, and stand-up comedy is no different. Just put yourself out there and start doing shows or open mics where you can work on your material in front of real audiences.

Keys to Great Comedy

The first key is timing. If something should be funny but arrives too soon or too late, it will not be funny. Timing has everything to do with how well something resonates with an audience, and those who practice timing do so by exercising their synapses.

Humans are remarkably capable of sequencing only a handful of muscle movements in parallel– lifting an arm, making a fist, opening your hand, and closing it again, but we can make thousands of these timed movements at the same time. There is no reason an actor cannot act while he or she exercises. It's only when the exercise is done "wrong" that it produces a terrible result, and there is no greater wrong than failing to hear the signal that sounds at precisely the right moment. In the case of a comedy routine, several signals must be heard at the same time.

One of these is the punchline. When you hear people telling jokes it can sometimes seem as though they're building up to something for far too long. When they eventually get to an amusing observation, it doesn't seem all that funny, because the punchline has been delayed too long. A comedian wants to build up a degree of tension before releasing it with the punchline, but it cannot be overly played.

The better the joke, the longer tension can be allowed to build. A comedian isn't likely to tell his audience something he doesn't think is funny! The problem is that this tension needs to be released at precisely the right moment or the punchline won't be funny.

This is where your brain comes in. You've heard the stories about people who have been struck by lightning and left with strange abilities. One person may suddenly find that they can move objects with their mind, another may have a kind of X-ray vision that allows them to see through walls, etc. But these are exceptional cases. Most people have no such capacity. However, if you train your synapses to react to certain stimuli, you will find that they react to other stimuli.

For example, when I was a teenager I heard the word "psychic" in a context that contained many of the signals that make people laugh. It began as a dull word but ended up with me laughing uncontrollably because of an uncontrollable impulse. I didn't realize what was happening until I went back and read what I'd written at the time.

Why did this work for me? Because, many years earlier as a child, my father had gathered together all the jokes he thought were funny and had shown them to me. As soon as my brain saw the word "psychic" it knew that's what I'd been told to find funny. My father told me one joke in this particular context, "What does a psychic do on Columbus Day?" When I heard this joke as a child, it made both of us laugh.

This means that there is no such thing as the "wrong" joke, and the more time that goes by before you deliver your punchline, the funnier it will be.

Humor is a matter of timing.

Another surprising thing about comedy is a joke can be funny because it relates to something that with which we are familiar. One example is an observation relating to reality television.

The best way to understand this is to think of something that has happened on the telly. Suppose you were watching an episode of Big Brother and some contestant said "Bit of a kinky one, ain't she!" If you know this is true about reality television, there's secret knowledge at work that can make you laugh. But what if the idea was just generalized from an everyday experience?

A great example of this comes from a very famous joke: "How many archaeologists does it take to change a light bulb? None, because archaeologists are too busy digging things up."

Consider what you know about archaeology. It's all about looking for buried remains. What if someone asks, "How many economists does it take to change a light bulb? None, because economists are too busy digging things up."

The only thing that's changed is the name of the profession. So why don't we find it funny? Because we know about archaeology and there's good reason to think that economics is an exact science. And that means that this joke depends on something non-rational.

What if they had asked, "How many biologists does it take to change a light bulb? None, because biologists are too busy looking at plants. And what about how many psychologists? None, because psychologists are too busy looking at people.

The joke is based on two observations of reality, one that most people will view as rational (that biologists are interested in plants) and another that is irrational (psychologists don't talk to each other). If you make a joke like this, you're probably going to get a reaction from your listeners because they've got two contradictory things running through their minds at once. When you tell something true about reality, it's bound to be true... or at least true in some sense. This is a joke that relies on the truth and absurdity of our reasoning errors.

The takeaway is that for you to be able to laugh at the absurdity of someone else's reasoning error, you have to know about it. If you don't know about it, then it will just seem stupid or fanciful to you. But if you know about it, then your brain can see that and react accordingly by making a connection between the two and seeing the humor.

CHAPTER 10: STORYTELLING

Storytelling is a time-honored way to make people laugh, whether through the use of jokes or clever wordplay. Sometimes laughter is difficult to come by and stories just don't seem funny at all.

Don't worry—we have some tips for you! Here are five ways to guarantee that your next story will be so hilarious that people won't stop laughing.

1. Start with an unpleasant situation.
2. Turn the tables on yourself (or someone else).
3. Confuse an innocent bystander with senseless words or actions.
4. Surprise your audience in an odd but pleasant manner—they may not believe at first that they're being laughed at.
5. Make fun of something that people take too seriously (See #3).

Here are some examples of where these stories would work well:

- You're about to meet a guy you don't know. As you're watching him from across the room, he suddenly collapses to the floor and foams at the mouth in pain. (This is great for audiences who are fond of practical jokes.)
- Your friend goes out with her hair parted differently than usual. When she returns, she tells you that while out, some guy said something rude about her hair and hit on her. (She's used to

getting teased. This is great for audiences who are timid about jokes.)

- Someone you know has a very odd name (See #2).
- You pick up a large, heavy object at the store. When you're just about to put it down, your friend walks into the room and asks if you could deliver his package to him. The box is too large and heavy for you to lift on your own, but it can fit in your pocket easily if you put it upside down.
- A friend asks you to pretend that he's your boss, then says something outrageous about him that could lead people to laugh.
- You see a guy eat five hot dogs at once. (This is great for audiences who like to gamble.)
- A friend of yours is constantly drunk, making him a prime target for practical jokes. (This is great for audiences who enjoy not going home alone.)
- A stranger walks up to you and says that you look familiar, though he's certain that he's never met you before. (This is fun for everyone because people love to be told they're recognizable. It's also good for audiences who want to tell jokes.)
- You're at a restaurant and you get a spicy kick from the food.
- You have a new car and your friends smoke cigarettes in it. Then they make fun of you.
- Your friend's new boyfriend previews the night ahead by e-mailing what the weather will be like, how he'll dress, and what he plans to do with his free time.
- You're in a foul mood, and you try to annoy people.

- Your friend keeps making fun of your new haircut. He says that he thought you looked better before. (This is great for audiences who are fond of hair jokes.)
- Someone asks you about an embarrassing event from the past that they witnessed.
- Your computer laughs when you feed it words in an incorrect order or say some strange things that shouldn't make sense. (This is good for audiences who like to be surprised.)
- A friend smells unpleasant and you ask him what he's been doing.
- You're at a party where someone tells you they used to live in a shoe.
- You go to a restaurant where the food isn't spicy enough for you.
- You take an elevator up to the office of your company's CEO.
- When someone asks you to fill them in on the details of your weekend, you tell them about the time you saw a guy eat his dog.
- You're at a party where someone plays loud music. You complain to your friends that everybody else seems to be having an awful time, but then they turn the music off and play some horrible opera music instead.
- You get into an argument with a friend. You tell him you don't know why he keeps doing things to annoy you and that he's making you mad.
- A friend of yours is constantly drunk and falling down. You walk him home but have a hard time convincing him not to drive his car.
- This one's special. It's a goof on the whole question-asking thing that all actors do in plays when they are trying out material.

You're talking to the drunk friend about getting in his car. He gets annoyed because you keep asking him if he's sure he wants to drive himself home.

- You're at a party where somebody has invited you to play a board game. You can't play well and you keep losing to other people.
- Your friend drives up to the restaurant in his new sports car as an old car passes by.
- You're at a party where someone talks a lot about themselves.
- You're at a restaurant with your family. Your children have been very naughty, and you've threatened to punish them, but you don't.
- Someone doesn't believe in ghosts, so you tell them a story about when you were younger your family went to some scary house in the woods that was supposed to be haunted. You see him get scared.
- You're at a party and one guy is telling you a story about his job. The story is boring, so you say things like, "Yeah, yeah, right," and count the ceiling tiles.
- A very rich man marries a woman because he likes her money and doesn't care that she's not beautiful.
- Someone has invited you to his house to see his expensive things. You touch them and drooling.
- A rich person wants to buy his daughter a very expensive doll for her birthday, but the doll costs $1,000 more than he has. He tells the clerk that he doesn't have enough money to pay for it, but if they can hold it for him until next week when he gets paid, he'll come back with the rest of the money. The clerk says yes.

The wealthy man goes home happy that his daughter will get her expensive doll after all. One week passes, and no one comes back to pay for the doll. The wealthy man calls the store. The clerk says it's against policy to hold an item for over one week, but he'll make an exception in this case because the wealthy man is a very good customer. "How much do I owe?" asks the wealthy man. "You don't owe us anything," says the clerk, "we're just holding it for you."

CHAPTER 11: PRACTICAL JOKES

Practical jokes have been a society staple for centuries. From the first time someone invited his gullible friend into that weird house, they passed on the way home from school and convinced him it's haunted, we have been relentlessly trying to fool each other.

But how do you come up with a fantastic prank? A practical joke is only as good as its punchline. Everyone has different tastes, so coming up with funny ideas can be difficult. That's why we've compiled six of the best tricks to make someone laugh—or maybe to just get even!

Invasion From Uranus

This is one of the more popular jokes around, and it works wonderfully well! The only problem with it is if you're looking to perform this joke on someone who already believes in aliens, it just won't work. If you still want to pull it off, you'll be doing so in good faith, and everyone will thank you for it!

Two Englishmen were walking along the beach... "I wonder what page we're on in the Alien Manual," said one. "I don't think we'll find out until we land," said the other, putting his feet in the ocean.

"So tell me about this new planet you've discovered," said a beautiful woman who was looking for her alien. "It's called Uranus." said the man. "So how do I get there?" she asked. The man shook his head sadly and said, "You're never going to make it as an alien."

Emo Prankster

When my brother was going through an emo phase, he would go down Main Street wearing torn black clothes and applying eyeliner to every inch of visible skin (he didn't know about bicep tattoos back then). Every time someone asked him what was wrong, he would cry and say "everything" in an anguished tone.

I use this joke about as often as I can. Whenever I'm feeling bored, or in need of a laugh, I'll just apply black lipstick and start crying outside Boots about how much my life sucks (this doesn't make me feel any better though). There are a few times where people genuinely think I'm upset about something... but that's not the point!

The Martians Are Coming! The Martians Are Coming!

Everyone knows that the government is hiding aliens from us. Martians, that is, which is why this joke works so well.

"I've just got word from the Institute for Extraterrestrial Research," said the scientist to his colleague in the laboratory. "The Martians are coming!" "Are you sure?" asked the other man. "Absolutely," said the scientist. "They're coming by bus. And they're bringing chlorophyll. We must have it."

Jesse Jaws

I'm not exactly sure where this joke came from, but I remember someone telling me about it at school once. The story goes that there was this shark that grew uncontrollably attached to a little girl. The shark followed her everywhere, and when she went swimming in the ocean one day, she became so afraid of the shark that she refused to go back to the water—even though her parents were begging her to.

This is basically what I do with my friends (or people I don't know very well) whenever they swim in my pool, I act like I can't see them. They flail their arms around pretending to swim and even get their feet wet before getting out of the pool. Most of the time they don't want to go back in, but I always support them!

The Human Flying Saucer

This is probably my favorite practical joke—and I can't believe it's not more popular. Basically, you ask someone if they'd like to be a human flying saucer. When they agree, you place food underneath them and tell them to hover over it while singing "We Will Rock You" by Queen (the original version). Then you throw a cushion at them! "Aah!" says the victim. "What was that? Did you just throw something at me?" "No! Sorry. It was my flying saucer!"

I prefer this joke to the Alien Manual one, but they're both great. The person who's the victim will usually be pretty freaking happy when you tell them, and will thank you for making their birthday a lot better!

The seven-year-old walks up to his mother in the supermarket and says: "Look, mommy. I found a new brand of toothpaste that doesn't have fluoride in it." "Why would you want that?" she asks. The child replies: "So I can get all the strong white teeth like Tom Cruise!"

Many people (myself included) always want to have teeth that are as white as their idols! If you ever meet a friend who does, don't be afraid to use this joke. It might be just the thing they need to hear!

I am your missing sock. I know where I belong. Please put me in the washer and dryer with my brothers and sisters.

This is one of the most useful jokes around (especially on wedding days). If you ever come across a pair of friends who have lost a sock, tell them that being lost is like being dead. To be honest, though, my choice for the most useful joke would probably go to: "If two people hate each other, does it matter how many witnesses they have?"

Finally, when I say that this is my "top 10" list of jokes... it's not actually what I think are the best ones. I'm just trying to cover as many bases as I can. This is only a list of my favorites, and it's not like I'll be telling all these jokes all the time. It's just something I wanted to share with you! Enjoy!

Be sure to check out the entire list of "Top 30 Jokes for Grown-Ups" too! If you're an adult, this is a great way to keep things interesting when you're out with your friends. And if you're a kid, please tell those funny adults that they should try some of these jokes out on you. You're not too young for a laugh!

By the way... although it may not always seem like it, I have a sense of humor. I hope you've found something in this list that you'll enjoy, or think about putting to good use. And if you have any other suggestions for jokes too, feel free to send them in! If they're good, I may just steal them from you and add them myself. Great! In that case, I've got one for you: "What did one ripped monkey say to the other?" "You look terrible!" (Sorry... no joke there, and it probably went without saying...)

Well, there's my list of "Top 30 Jokes for Grown-Ups." To be honest, it's probably not all that great. But at least I thought about the jokes (still funny if you ask me)! If you've got any suggestions for jokes that you think might make this list better, don't forget to send them in!

Keep on laughing guys! Don't thank me for the silly comments you'll find below. There are 12.5 billion people on the planet... so that'll make for a lot of funny comments!

CHAPTER 12: SITUATION COMEDY

Situation comedy relies on a network of humorous characters. It usually consists of short storylines, plot, and dialogue. The story is told via a series of scenes that have the same basic setup or punch line. It's about as simple as they come in terms of comedy presentation, but it's hard to argue with its effectiveness!

Situation comedy probably has its roots in the ancient Greek vaudeville shows. Comedy emerged from this tradition as an integral part of performance art. In turn, situation comedies are descended from traditions such as pantomime or variety shows with singing and dancing or juggling.

Situation comedy remains one of the most popular and successful forms of entertainment in modern culture. Many classic sitcoms are rerun on television every day and have found their way into the hearts of entire generations. New situation comedies continue to be made and actors get better pay and do less work!

Sitcoms are like action adventures in terms of their storyline or premise, except that they're much easier to watch than action adventures. They rarely have complicated plots.

Most situation comedy scenarios are so simple they could have been written by children. The characters are stereotypical, simplistic and the plot is often simple-minded. This makes them easy to follow for the most casual viewer.

Frequently, situations in situations comedies seem very real. There are usually horrible secrets that have been hidden from the main character which they eventually learn about and try to deal with, usually resulting in a misunderstanding and a farcical reaction from friends and family.

The best situation comedies will have a wacky character who is a direct contrast to the main character. Usually, this person will be used in a series of comedic scenes that take place in various locations, typically in places off-limits for the main character.

They're usually used as a form of "breaking the fourth wall" where the main character will talk directly to the audience, often using a kind of surrealistic or over-the-top confession or explanation for something that's going on in their life. Most situation comedies have this sort of "confessional" element built into their storyline which makes them interesting to watch and easy to follow.

Situation comedies rely on an array of common situations for their humor, such as "man-on-the-street interviews" or minor incidents that happen in everyday life. The characters are used to entertain us with their reactions and thoughts about these things. The comedy comes from the simple way characters react to these incidents or situations just as they might in real life.

Sitcoms can be watched for laughs by anyone who is a fan of situation comedies—men, women, children—everyone is entertained by them! The best situation comedies are very easy on the eyes and ears as well!

Many sitcoms have a major international following and are quite popular in multiple countries around the world.

Cable networks like HBO or Showtime specialize in these programs. It's probably the easiest way to break into the entertainment industry without going to Hollywood. Sitcoms follow no specific style. They've been made for decades and some of the best are still in re-runs today.

If you're an aspiring television writer, you can make a sitcom as well! It's one of the top ways to get your name out there and get more work for future projects.

Sitcoms are a form of entertainment that help people relax and just laugh. Even if you're not into television, you will find that following sitcoms can be hilarious!

Usually, a situation comedy is made in front of a live audience and focuses on the actions and thoughts of the characters being portrayed by the actors in a continuous storyline or theme. Some things that happen are also things that may happen to you in real life, although most sitcom situations are highly exaggerated! Most of them are set in familiar household surroundings, so you don't need a university degree to understand what's happening.

CHAPTER 13: SKETCH COMEDY

Sketch comedy is a type of comedic performance designed to imitate situations or people humorously. It was developed around the same time as silent films.

There is no single, definitive definition for sketch comedy, but it can generally be described as humor "played" in long-form. It is typically scripted, character-driven and plot-based, often satirical or absurdist, and usually improvisational with plenty of room for more than one performer.

Sketch comedy is sometimes used interchangeably with the term variety show, particularly when discussing shows that mix comedy sketches with musical entertainment, such as Saturday Night Live. Sketch comedy uses an interplay of visual and verbal humor. It can be performed in sketch or long-form, with or without music, and on stage, film, or television. Performance formats include concerts, stand-up shows, variety shows, cabarets, and skits. Sometimes they are presented as part of a larger theatrical performance featuring other performers such as magicians, illusionists, and musicians.

The parody is a very basic structure on which almost every sketch comedy program is based. Parody sketches are brief and feature performers imitating characters or situations from well-known films or television shows. The characters are presented in a way that makes them seem like caricatures or exaggerated versions of the source material. Sometimes, even a real-world performer will appear with a character based on themselves. As in any sketch comedy, many of these "characters" are stock characters. One of the most popular sources for this type of sketch is political satire and "Saturday Night Live" has had an especially long tradition of parodying political figures and events.

Performed as early as the 1700s in music halls all over Europe and America, skit comedy was popularized by theater impresario Fred Karno who assembled large troupes to perform his string of hit shows including "A Night Out." Karno performers were noted for their rough and tumble physical humor. Many sketches were quick, one-off jokes or lampoons of current events.

Karno's comedy involved actors chomping on cigars and crunching down on hard candy while making humorous, loud noises. This was due, in part, to the lack of microphones and amplification available to performers at the time. Another staple of British sketch comedy is the music hall tradition, a series of acts performing a range of comic songs, monologues, or brief sketches with minimal props (or none). The acts usually finalized on the day of the show, so a new routine was often written specifically for that night. This resulted in a completely original act for each performance.

Within 30 years of Karno's death, the music hall tradition was well-established across Britain and America. However, at this point most of these shows were no longer recorded, so they have almost completely vanished from history.

American stage performers Richard Pryor and Bill Cosby built their popularity on performances that featured both live-action and short comedy skits mixed in with their stand-up comedy routines. Besides their skits, Pryor and Cosby also performed stand-up comedy sets that lasted only a half-hour or less. These short stand-up routines also appeared in their early comedy albums.

In the United States, the term vaudeville refers to a sophisticated stage variety show featuring comedic skits and other entertainments. It was popular from the early 1880s until the 1920s. The word is French for "forget-me-not", a flower that is a symbol of true love. During this period, skits were allowed an audience time to settle in before a featured performance (usually a song or dance). Often this was interspersed with short films or performances by buffoons.

The vaudeville revival began in the 1980s with a surge of interest in vintage stage comedy. The most famous revivals include those of the Theatrical Syndicate, the International Vaudeville Club, and the Vaudéville Manager's Association.

Sketch-based cartoons appeared on American television as early as 1941 in the form of "animated interludes" between programs. They were the first broadcast on NBC from June 12, 1941, to September 1942, when they moved to CBS from 1943 to 1944. They were produced by Wallace V. Redstone's Gulf+Western Film Corporation company animation department under Paul Terry's supervision.

In the 1980s, the Canadian sketch comedy series SCTV aired, which became enormously popular in Canada and subsequently in the U.S. The show followed a similar format as "Saturday Night Live" but featured more obscure parodies and writing from Phil Hartman (who later joined SNL). It was canceled after 6 seasons when many of its cast members left to join SNL (e.g., John Candy, Joe Flaherty, Eugene Levy,

Martin Short), while others who did not (i.e., Andrea Martin and Catherine O'Hara) returned to the show for the final season. One episode featured a cast member winning a lip-sync battle against "American Idol" winner Kris Allen.

After the final SCTV season in 1986, John Candy, who had left the series, unhappy with his salary, returned to the show as an executive producer and helped assemble new talent with the help of some of the SCTV veterans (e.g., Martin, O'Hara). Some of the new performers (such as Dave Thomas), however, could not gain a following and found success elsewhere, leaving without appearing on any new episodes. Only O'Hara was able to make it from SCTV to another television project ("Wings"), in which she portrayed Richard Nixon's wife. Some performers, such as Dave Thomas and Rick Moranis, continued to have success on SCTV alumni projects (e.g., "The Bob & Doug McKenzie Show", which they created with Thomas' brother Pat, and Dan Aykroyd).

SCTV birthed the careers of several later famous comedians including Bill Murray (who got his start on the show at age 20), Harold Ramis, John Candy, Catherine O'Hara, and Joe Flaherty. Second City alumni who also appeared regularly on SCTV included Eugene Levy, Andrea Martin, Martin Short, Robin Duke, and Tony Rosato.

SCTV was an early showcase for the theatrical antics of John Candy and Eugene Levy. Candy would frequently impersonate Canadian singer-songwriter Neil Young. In one sketch, he broke into the Stadacona Studio 54 and shouted "Fire!" (in a manner reminiscent of Young's legendary late-1970s concert visits to Toronto). Levy would go on to make a name for himself as a leading comedy actor in the 1980s with his portrayal of over-the-top character Doug McKenzie (and later Brent

Butt), co-starring with Dave Thomas as the McKenzie Brothers on their TV show, "The Great White North."

The show ran for 186 episodes, from 1976 to 1980 before going on hiatus, and had a record-breaking 297 prime-time reruns on CBC Television from 1980 to 1987. The show was syndicated to hundreds of U.S. TV stations by 1986, and several foreign markets (such as Brazil) aired the show uncut and unedited, in direct defiance of CBC's wishes.

In 2018 it was announced that producer Scott Aukerman would host a new comedy show for Netflix called "Comedy Originals." The first season centers on "Aukerman's deranged characters, confusing stories about his childhood, his parents, and their sexual exploits."

These original sketches have been adapted to movies, television series, video-games, stage shows, and video games.

CHAPTER 14: SOCIAL MEDIA AND INTERNET

Take advantage of your skills on the Internet by making funny videos, writing funny posts, posting photos of you doing something humorous. Have a business of your own? Turn your work into content for different social media accounts.

- Pick one network and stick with it, keeping all the posts you do on that network locally.
- Post every day, or at least 5 days out of the week, but try not to post too close together, which allow people's feed time to fill up before they see your content again.
- Find other like-minded individuals and reach out to them by following and commenting on their posts as well as creating original content for them to *like*.
- Mix media types: video, photos, articles, etc.
- Keep updates relevant, interesting, and engaging.
- Use hashtags to keep people up to date with your posts.
- Use photos of yourself or comical photos of others.
- If you are a business owner, turn your work into content for other social media accounts.

I could have done more research on how social media works and where I should post but I started posting content whenever it felt right and was fun. I post at least once per day, depending on my mood. The only time I don't post is during the middle of the school week, or if I'm camping or hiking somewhere. I have been posting on Facebook, Twitter, Instagram, and Snapchat, but my focus is the Facebook and Instagram accounts that were created for this research project.

In picking a network to use, they are all very similar in what they offer for free except for Snapchat. My first thought was that no one uses Snapchat anymore, but I have friends who use it. Instagram is my favorite because it has all the filters I use most, plus that's where my friends are, and who knows if you are going to be friends with everyone? Snapchat has instant messaging, which is great for sending a quick message. Instagram and Facebook do not allow private messaging, but they can let you know what someone likes or your friend's birthdate.

For followers, the most popular social media page was Facebook, followed by Instagram. I do not know why there was such an enormous difference in this section of the survey, but I'm sure others will share their thoughts about it. I believe Instagram is the next Facebook in terms of popularity. Facebook has a huge user base, but people are getting bored with it, so now they are looking for other options like Instagram and Snapchat.

One thing I wished I knew more about would be how to create a specific network or business page for different networks, such as Instagram or even Snapchat. I also believe my followers would like me to post more frequently than once per day, if possible, since it's not every day that you find something worth sharing or something as good as gold. It would also help to respond to other's posts because sometimes there are relevant posts that deserve a quick response. If you do not respond to their post, they will think your brand is inactive and that there's no point in following you.

I would also like to know more about the hashtags, even though I have been using them I still do not know what they are for. They are helpful for interacting with other posts and getting your posts noticed by others. Instagram is all about the hashtag, and when people search them it brings up a list of pictures, if yours is one of them then you will get more views on your photos and hopefully new followers. For social media marketing, hashtags are a great way to gain more followers and get more likes on your posts. I do not use hashtags because I have enough followers and I don't want anymore, but for those who have a small audience, this can be useful information.

I learned Snapchat users are more likely than others to use filters or create a story. They also prefer posting pictures over videos. With Snapchat, it is all about creating stories and making memories. Instagram is picture-heavy, and not as much about the story as Snapchat, so they stay less personalized. It is all about selfies, what you are doing, and what you are wearing. When it comes to Facebook, I honestly don't think they even use it.

To get more views, I would suggest people publicize their content, share their posts on other social media sites, and keep the content current with interactions and new updates. My followers need to know that I will always respond to them personally. It can be stressful for them when they send me a message and don't get a response. It is what makes me a little sad that I do not respond to them as much as I would like.

Getting more followers means there will be more people who want to talk with you. You might even start noticing it is hard to keep up with everything, so try using other accounts to help you out.

The school week was kind of difficult because I always wanted to respond to people, but the most important thing in this project was getting the feelings out of my head and being able to sleep at night.

CHAPTER 15: PEOPLE DON'T LAUGH AT YOUR JOKES—WHAT TO DO?

Nobody is laughing at my jokes, and I want to know what to do about it!

A good comedian knows not to take a joke too seriously. The only person who thinks your jokes are funny is you. It's important to remember that the people you're telling your jokes to are only laughing because they're trying to be polite or give you a second chance. That's why they're not laughing.

As a comedian, it's your job to make those people laugh! Maybe your jokes aren't funny, but it doesn't matter. You're there to entertain them and make them forget their troubles for a few minutes. You might not be funny, but you still have to perform because it's show business.

Enthusiasm Counts—Believe It or Not!

If you don't believe your joke is funny to the crowd, don't worry about it. Just try to make the crowd laugh, anyway. Don't tell yourself that you're not funny, just have fun and keep telling jokes.

If you don't take your comedy seriously, then no one else will either. You realize that being a comedian is just a job like any other job. If you do it right, then it can be very rewarding and you'll love every minute!

But if you take yourself too seriously, then your comedy act will fail. Be happy and enjoy making people laugh!

A great comedian knows how to adapt their show to the audience. This means you should not tell the same jokes you used to tell your high-school classmates, unless they are in the audience. Even they don't find it funny anymore. Tell jokes that people your age like, and they will laugh even harder.

If Your Jokes Aren't Working–Change 'Em!

Maybe your jokes aren't working because they're stale. Work some new material into your act.

When a comedian realizes that his or her jokes aren't working, and they know there is nothing they can do about it, it's time to end their set and go home. You should not stay out on the stage for the rest of your show if you're not bringing anything new to the table.

Routine Too Long–Tell a Story!

If you're telling a long joke, try interspersing a story between the joke parts. Most of the information you need to tell your joke comes from other sources, anyway.

A story is well-timed if you combine it with a joke. This is very important because you should never tell a story without a punch line. A joke is funny because it's ridiculous, but a story can be fun too if you make something out of nothing!

A Great Joke Focuses on Your Audience—Remember: They're Laughing at You!

You know your audience is laughing at you because they're laughing at your jokes, and you're still doing them, anyway. So why give up? Have fun with it! It's your job to entertain them, and you'll do that by making them laugh.

If you're a good comedian, then you'll love performing for people in the audience. They're still laughing at you but at least you're having fun doing it! If your routine is bad, they don't care about your act anymore. They only want to go home. So get out there and start telling jokes!

If You Get Stuck With Bad Jokes—Take a Joke Break!

Don't worry if some of your jokes aren't working out. There's always a new joke or two waiting in the wings that are just as good as any other joke in your act. You should not get discouraged about it. Just go on with your jokes and try to tell them as best as you can.

When you come up with a poor joke, just drop it out of your act. You don't have to keep doing it if the audience doesn't like it. It's much better than ignoring the fact that the joke doesn't work and continuing to tell it every time you go up on stage. Nobody is going to laugh at it anyway, so just cut your losses and move along!

CHAPTER 16: FEED YOUR BRAIN

Feed your brain with some hilariously witty quotes. Laugh, and learn what makes people tick. Enjoy, and maybe even learn what you can do to make people laugh too!

Some say laughter is the best medicine. We couldn't agree more! There are plenty of circumstances in life that can cause stress or sadness–making us feel like we need some laughter to lighten the mood. By helping others feel better using humor, we're giving back just a little in return for all those times we've chuckled at someone else's joke or gut-busting take on current events.

But it's hard to make people laugh and joke around at the same time. We all have our unique sense of humor, and we reach for jokes or situations that make us think "I said something funny!" Here are some great websites where you can read lots of funny things–articles, quotes, cartoons, jokes–to help you enhance your hilarious banter. Some quick tips:

- Take the time to laugh at your friends' jokes. They'll appreciate it every time!
- Go present-shopping for someone who makes you laugh (but doesn't require an expensive present). A CD, a book full of funny quotes, or some funny signs could brighten their day.

- Be genuinely interested in what others have to say. Ask what makes them laugh, or share a joke they might like. Be friendly. It'll make jokes and conversations flow much easier. Write down the best of your jokes so you can use them later—don't force yourself to be funny all the time! Let your natural humor take over when the mood strikes you, and you'll find it's easier to keep people laughing at your jokes than if you try too hard.

Now that you're ready to make people laugh, here are a few fun websites we found online—if you know of any others, please add them in the comments!

- The Cutting Room Floor has a great selection of funny quotes categorized by topic. If you like something you read on this site, click through to the author's site for more humor and jokes.
- When You Can't Get to Sleep is a great blog filled with fun facts about sleep. It's a quick read that will help you relax at night.
- Practical Joke Supply offers many fun things to wake others up with a laugh, including fake bugs and animals, funny emergency signs, and even paraffin wax droppings to fool motion sensor lights.
- We were tickled pink (ha!) by the pickle stories on www.FunnyPickle.com Read up on the history of pickles or read some funny signs to display in your pickle shop. (Oh no! The puns!)
- The Daily Joke is a blog kept current with a new joke every day. The site's focus is on legal jokes and law humor, but there's plenty of random humor too.

- For some lighter reading about North American science and nature, try Radar Magazine. Many of the articles are funny, and some are downright hilarious.
- The Onion website–an American satirical newspaper–has several funny articles, including one in which a man claims to have discovered a cure for AIDS that the government's keeping secret, a regimen of good diet and exercise.
- Hasbro Magazine is full of fun games and toys, and it's also pretty funny if you're into having fun. Plenty of silly jokes and puns here!
- Revolutionary Times is an impressive site for political humor–mostly from the conservative side of things, but still funny! If you prefer something with more liberal leanings, try Daily Kos.

CHAPTER 17: CREATING DEEPER CONNECTIONS

Creating deeper connections and developing rapport with people makes your daily life easier, and it's one of the most important things that you can do for yourself. It can make you happier and healthier and better able to enjoy your friendships, work relationships, family connections, and more.

A big part of creating rapport is being able to make people laugh. If you can create genuine laughter with someone, even in a short amount of time, then you've already built a firm foundation for friendship.

One of the biggest complaints that I hear from people who want to become more confident socially is that they feel awkward and uncomfortable around others. When they become more social, they enjoy themselves and have fun, but they're also afraid what they're saying might be perceived as stupid, inappropriate, or boring. They can't relax because they're constantly worried about what everyone else thinks of them.

One of the best ways to make people feel comfortable and at ease around you is to make them laugh. If you can do that, their guard comes down and they respond to you naturally instead of putting on a 'social face'. And once you've made someone laugh, it's just a brief step to sharing more personal information with them.

Tips About How to Make People Laugh

Be Playful

Look for opportunities to play around and have fun. You don't have to be silly all the time, but if there's an opportunity for some lightheartedness, definitely seize it. It doesn't matter what your jokes are about or how well they're received, and it doesn't matter if the people around you think they're funny. All that matters is that you're having fun and being playful.

If possible, try to do this in public places that aren't the scene of social situations. This will help keep you from getting too nervous or self-conscious, especially if it's someone you've just met. The risk of being judged or laughed at is much lower when there are other people around, and it's not a situation where strangers are hanging out in the same room.

If you don't feel like going out to play around, then grab some paper and get writing! Get creative and make up jokes to share with others. I have a lot of fun writing jokes and sharing them with friends. It's a great way to become comfortable with constructive criticism. Eventually, you'll find that most people don't care how funny your particular joke is, it just matters that you're having a good time and making others feel the same way too.

Share Stories That Are Silly or Playful

A Court Jester is an example of someone who successfully creates laughter by using stories. If you aren't ready for jokes yet, then just tell your story, and see if there's anything in it that can be viewed as silly or playful.

For example, you can tell a story about something that happened to you that turns out well. Follow this with a story where something happens in your life and it doesn't turn out so well. The two stories blend seamlessly and become one fun tale. You can also create humor from everyday situations by sharing a funny memory that you've had (or even made up). It's hard to be self-deprecating if others aren't laughing with you, so the more people are laughing with you, the better it is.

Ask Interesting Questions

Here's a simple, but effective tip for making people laugh. Ask interesting questions. Whenever you're talking to someone new, always have a few questions up your sleeve, and use them when the time is right. This takes away the pressure of deciding what to say and gives you something interesting to talk about.

You don't have to ask questions that are that interesting or unique, just make sure that they make sense and that it's clear that you're interested in knowing the answers. For example, if someone says "I used to live in New York City" then you could say "Oh, really? What was it like?" That's a good question to ask. It's not interesting, but it is an attempt to get more details. You're interested in finding out more about the other person and you're asking about their life.

Another great way to ask questions is to use what the person has already said. For example, if someone tells you they live in a big city, then say "Oh I didn't enjoy living in that city!"

Be Vulnerable and Self-Aware

When you begin with humor and fun, it's can be difficult to see where the line is between being playful and being foolish. The easiest thing to do is to just ask that question. When you're telling a story, try asking "but what if..." and see if you can turn the story around and make it funny.

You don't have to be self-deprecating, but it's a good idea to admit that you're human and vulnerable. The best way to do this is by finding situations where people will laugh at you. For example, ask yourself, "how can I make myself seem funny or unique?" Then go for it. See what happens when you take a risk. Also, try telling your personal stories in such a way that others are rooting for you... people will find it very appealing.

Use Body Language, Gestures, and Exaggerations

If you have a unique characteristic or habit that you can exaggerate for humor (for example, if you twitch a little when you're nervous), then use it in your jokes and stories. For example, if someone says "I like bugs" then you might say "I like bugs too... but I don't want them anywhere near me." That's hilarious because it's so contradictory.

Another option is to point at something while speaking with your hands facing outwards. For example, saying "I'm gonna go take a nap now" could be turned into "I'm going to go take a nap now... and I'll be out in the open. You can watch me, but you can't touch me." That's pretty funny... use your body language to drive a joke, and you'll see.

Practice Your Delivery

Your delivery is the most important part of any joke or story that you tell. If you're talking with someone new and it doesn't seem like they're getting what you're saying, then double-check your tone of voice and delivery because it's important they understand what you're saying. If it seems like they aren't understanding something, then try rephrasing your sentences for clarity (slow down if things are moving too fast). If they still don't get it, try another approach. For example, use more action words like "I'll", "you'll", or "we'll" in your sentences. These are all key phrases that tell people exactly what you're going to do.

If you're not good at body language, then another way to practice is role-play acting exercises. For example, imagine that you're talking to a person on the phone and you want them to laugh at one of your jokes. You can practice your jokes by saying them repeatedly until you feel pretty confident about how they sound and look good when delivered. Then try it out on a friend.

Practice Both Your Delivery and Your Facial Expressions

If you're serious about improving your delivery, then make sure you practice by doing a few simple things, such as listening to the way you speak, repeating what you say out loud, and trying out different ways of saying it. Also, watch videos of people delivering jokes or stories online and try to copy the best parts of their delivery.

CONCLUSION

Most of us enjoy a good laugh, or at the very least, the people that we're laughing with. Surprisingly, there is a science to being funny. We've broken down several simple ways to make people laugh—without even trying!

- **Be genuine about your feelings**: This way people will believe you are laughing with them. You can also use humor as a defense mechanism against embarrassment.
- **Use self-deprecating humor**: Since everyone's favorite person is themselves (aside from maybe infants), it's always funny when someone else points out their flaws and laughs along with them.
- **Bring others in on your humor**: Try adding unexpected characters to your humor! You can add a few people into the fun or add everyone together as one big joke!
- **Tell a story**: This way, you can do more than just tell a funny joke. It also allows you to include many characters and plot twists.
- **Be unpredictable**: Being unpredictable is a great way to get people laughing at freakish events and things that they wouldn't expect. If they know what you're going to say before it happens, then it'll lose its shock factor and the person won't be as entertained by it.

- **Use a specific type of humor**: The more specific your humor is, the funnier it will be to everyone. You can also add elements of surprise so that even people who know what to expect can't plan for the next part.
- **Make people laugh by being funny**: This is a joke, but it's also true! You can make yourself laugh at your jokes, make them into a comedy act, and connect with your audience on a more personal level... even if you're not that funny.
- **Use the bad guy archetype**: This is the same idea as the above, except used to make your jokes even more effective. If you're a person who takes extreme measures to stop people from laughing at your jokes, then you can probably guarantee that everyone will die laughing!
- **Think outside of the box**: Not necessarily literally, but the idea of what is within a box. Try making jokes that are way more ridiculous than you think possible. You might be surprised at how funny they are!
- **Be a superb storyteller**: This one ties everything together. Make sure that every single bit of humor has a beginning, middle, and an end, so that it all flows together into one big story. Be sure to tell it as if you're living the story!
- **Have a story that no one will believe**: This is similar to the above, except it's more exciting. Make an unbelievable joke seem like it happened. It can be as simple as having someone tell their anecdote, or you can make something up that your audience might think is true... but isn't.
- **Have some characters in your humor**: This way, you'll have a few people to experiment with and make fun of–like those

comedy movies where there's a variety of people who are all making jokes about each other and then taking turns roasting each other!

- **Play up to your audience**: You can make people laugh by playing into whatever stereotypes your audience may have about you. For example, if a group of women is laughing at you, act very feminine and make fun of yourself.
- **Ask for the mike**: Another way to mess with people is to ask for the mic (or just walk up and take it from them if they're not using it). By doing this, you can get rid of their self-imposed restrictions on what they do and don't say, and then let them have it!
- **Use puns**: Puns are an effective way to make people laugh. They're also a good way to start any sort of humor. You can get a few puns in and move from there to whatever else you'd like to say.
- **Be annoying**: This will get people laughing because annoyance is funny when it's done on purpose! Just be careful that you do nothing that could cause physical harm.
- **Be ridiculous:** This can be a little tricky, but you can make your humor completely ridiculous. This kind of humor takes practice and isn't funny to most people until they've heard it done a few times... but then when it gets funny, everyone will laugh!
- **Be creative**: You might discover that you don't have any excellent jokes that you can use for your humor. That's OK! Sometimes not having the best jokes means you need to make something work instead of coming up with something new. You can even draw ideas from other things as long as they aren't directly related to what you're trying to achieve.

Funny Quotes for Laughs

Sometimes you just have to add a little humor to your life, whether it be to brighten up your day or make things easier for you overall. When that happens, there's nothing more useful than funny quotes–unless maybe they're from a cartoon character. Either way, here are some good examples of humorous quotes that you might find funny!

"I don't know what the key to success is, but the key to failure is trying to please everyone,"–Bill Cosby.

"I need someone really bad... Are you really bad? If not, then pass me by,"–Snoop Dogg.

"Always remember that you are absolutely unique. Just like everyone else,"–Margaret Mead.

"Even if you're on the right track, you'll get run over if you just sit there,"–Will Rogers.

"If at first you don't succeed, then skydiving definitely isn't for you,"–Henry David Thoreau.

CPSIA information can be obtained
at www.ICGtesting.com
Printed in the USA
BVHW041126060721
611236BV00017B/545

9 781914 161346